# Written by Neil Morris

## Cartoons by Mark Davis

M i L e s
K e L L y
PUBLISHING

**Projects created by**
Ting Morris

**Art direction**
Clare Sleven

**Design**
Mackerel Design

**Project management**
Mark Darling

**Artwork commissioned by**
Lynne French, Susanne Grant, Natasha Smith

**Art reference**
Lesley Cartlidge, Liberty Mella

**Editorial director**
Paula Borton

First published in 2000 by
Miles Kelly Publishing Ltd
Bardfield Centre, Great Bardfield, Essex CM7 4SL
Reprinted 2001

2468109753

British Library Cataloguing-in-Publication Data
A catalogue record for this book is available from the British Library

ISBN 1-90294-735-5

Printed in Hong Kong

**Acknowledgements**

The publishers wish to thank the following artists who have contributed to
this book:
Mike Foster (Maltings Partnership), Janos Marffy, Annabel Milne,
Tracey Morgan (B.L. Kearley Ltd), Martin Sanders, Mike Saunders.

The publishers wish to thank the following sources for the photographs
used in this book:
Corbis: Page 43 (TL)
All other photographs from Miles Kelly Archives.

e-mail: info@mileskelly.net
www.mileskelly.net

# CONTENTS

# PARTS OF THE BODY

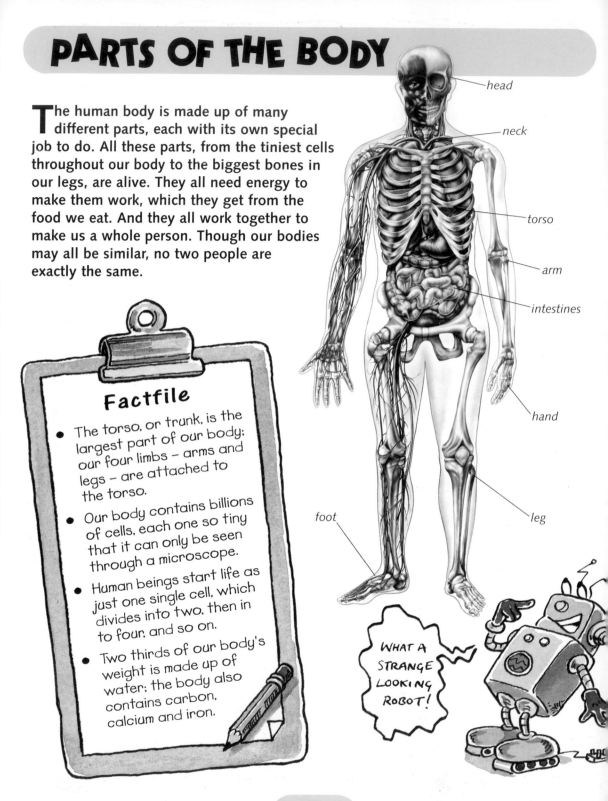

The human body is made up of many different parts, each with its own special job to do. All these parts, from the tiniest cells throughout our body to the biggest bones in our legs, are alive. They all need energy to make them work, which they get from the food we eat. And they all work together to make us a whole person. Though our bodies may all be similar, no two people are exactly the same.

head

neck

torso

arm

intestines

hand

leg

foot

## Factfile

- The torso, or trunk, is the largest part of our body; our four limbs – arms and legs – are attached to the torso.

- Our body contains billions of cells, each one so tiny that it can only be seen through a microscope.

- Human beings start life as just one single cell, which divides into two, then in to four, and so on.

- Two thirds of our body's weight is made up of water; the body also contains carbon, calcium and iron.

WHAT A STRANGE LOOKING ROBOT!

4

# Quiz

1. Where in the body is our brain?

2. What is the name of the joint between the arm and hand?

3. How many digits do we have?

4. Human beings are mammals – true or false?

5. What is the central part of a human cell called?

6. Are we warm-blooded or cold-blooded?

# Body shapes

1. To draw body shapes, you need a big sheet of paper and a friend. Lie face-up on the paper and ask your friend to draw around you with a pencil.

2. Colour in the body with paint and cut out the shape. Glue on eyes, nose, mouth and strips of paper for hair.

3. Draw your friend's shape in the same way. Then you can put your bodies up on the wall. Do they look the same?

# SKELETON

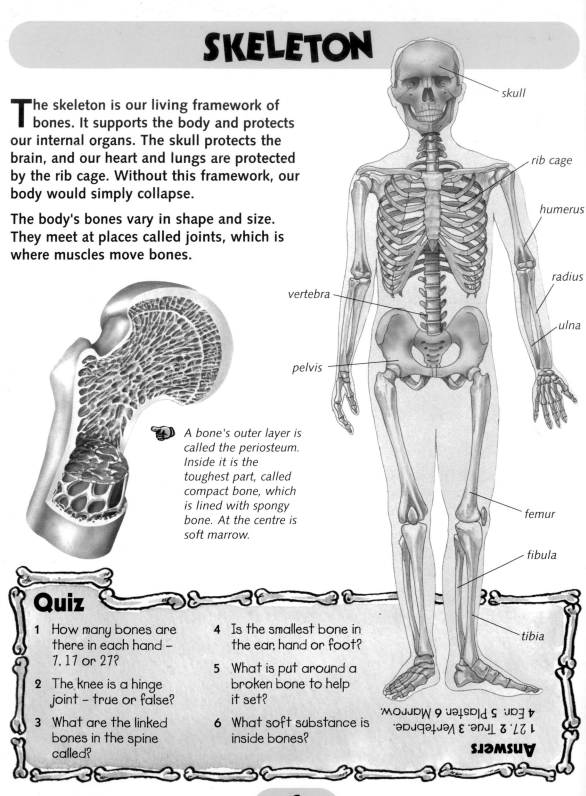

The skeleton is our living framework of bones. It supports the body and protects our internal organs. The skull protects the brain, and our heart and lungs are protected by the rib cage. Without this framework, our body would simply collapse.

The body's bones vary in shape and size. They meet at places called joints, which is where muscles move bones.

A bone's outer layer is called the periosteum. Inside it is the toughest part, called compact bone, which is lined with spongy bone. At the centre is soft marrow.

skull

rib cage

humerus

radius

ulna

vertebra

pelvis

femur

fibula

tibia

## Quiz

1  How many bones are there in each hand – 7, 17 or 27?

2  The knee is a hinge joint – true or false?

3  What are the linked bones in the spine called?

4  Is the smallest bone in the ear, hand or foot?

5  What is put around a broken bone to help it set?

6  What soft substance is inside bones?

## Factfile

- An adult has about 206 bones.

- Babies are born with as many as 270 bones; as a child grows, some bones join together.

- The hips and shoulders are called ball-and-socket joints, because that's what they look like and how they work.

- You may be up to a centimetre shorter in the evening than when you wake up in the morning; your spine squashes up slightly as you stand during the day.

- The femur, or thigh bone, is the body's largest bone, making up over a quarter of a person's height.

YOU CAN SEE WHICH IS THE LARGEST BONE IN MY BODY!

# Wired-up bones

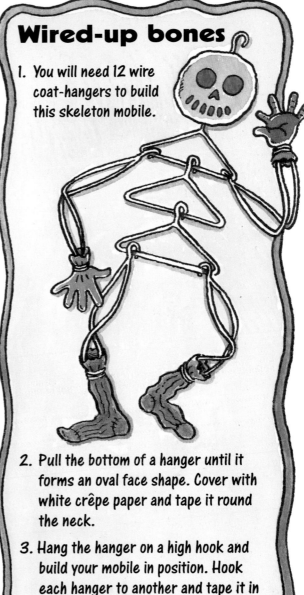

1. You will need 12 wire coat-hangers to build this skeleton mobile.

2. Pull the bottom of a hanger until it forms an oval face shape. Cover with white crêpe paper and tape it round the neck.

3. Hang the hanger on a high hook and build your mobile in position. Hook each hanger to another and tape it in place. Hook arm hangers to the shoulders and tape on old gloves. Hook foot hangers to the legs and pull on stuffed socks.

4. Draw a face on the crêpe. If you want to make it really creepy, spray your skeleton with white or luminous paint.

# MUSCLES

To run or jump, we use our muscles. In fact, muscles make all our body's movements possible, even tiny ones such as blinking or smiling. To do this, muscles shorten and pull on the bones to which they are attached.

Some of our muscles work automatically, without us thinking about it. These include the chest muscles that help us breathe and the muscles in the stomach and intestines that help us digest food.

WOW, D'YOU THINK I'VE GOT ALL THOSE MUSCLES?

## Factfile

- The human body has about 620 muscles that it uses for movement.

- You use about 200 muscles every time you take a single step.

- The tiny muscles that help our eyes focus move about 100,000 times a day; you would have to walk about 80 km to give your leg muscles that much exercise.

- More than 30 small muscles in our face allow us to smile, frown and make other expressions.

Muscles work in pairs, such as the biceps and triceps in your upper arm.

triceps

biceps

**1**

To lift something, the biceps muscle gets shorter.

**2**

The hinge joint of the elbow moves.

**3**

To move the arm back down, the triceps shortens and the biceps gets longer.

# Quiz

1 Which muscles are stronger, jaw muscles or calf muscles?

2 We have quadriceps as well as biceps and triceps – true or false?

3 Which large muscle is the gluteus maximus?

4 Do muscles make up 3%, 30% or 90% of the body?

5 Where is the deltoid muscle?

6 Can you tear a muscle?

**Answers**
1 Jaw muscles. 2 True. 3 The buttock. 4 30%. 5 In the shoulder. 6 Yes (athletes sometimes do).

THE BIGGEST MUSCLES ARE THE BUTTOCKS!

# Tug of war

1. To play this muscly game, make up two equal teams – it could be just one on each side.

2. Grab the ends of a strong rope, take up the strain till the rope is taught, and then try to pull each other an agreed distance (say, 2 m).

3. If you are losing, don't let go of the rope. If you did, your opponent would go flying backwards and this could be very dangerous.

# BODY ORGANS

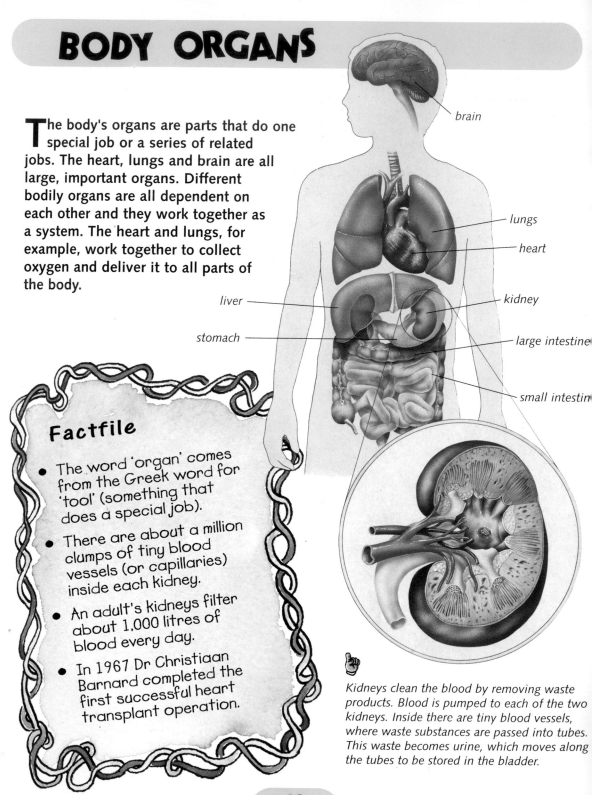

The body's organs are parts that do one special job or a series of related jobs. The heart, lungs and brain are all large, important organs. Different bodily organs are all dependent on each other and they work together as a system. The heart and lungs, for example, work together to collect oxygen and deliver it to all parts of the body.

brain

lungs

heart

liver

kidney

stomach

large intestine

small intestine

## Factfile

- The word 'organ' comes from the Greek word for 'tool' (something that does a special job).

- There are about a million clumps of tiny blood vessels (or capillaries) inside each kidney.

- An adult's kidneys filter about 1,000 litres of blood every day.

- In 1967 Dr Christiaan Barnard completed the first successful heart transplant operation.

Kidneys clean the blood by removing waste products. Blood is pumped to each of the two kidneys. Inside there are tiny blood vessels, where waste substances are passed into tubes. This waste becomes urine, which moves along the tubes to be stored in the bladder.

# Quiz

1 What are our organs of sight called?

2 How many times is our blood cleaned every day by the kidneys – 3, 30 or 300 times?

3 What is a person who gives an organ to someone else called?

4 Scientists are experimenting with using pigs' hearts for human transplants – true or false?

5 Can an artificial kidney machine do the job of damaged kidneys?

6 Which organ makes bile?

**Answers**
1 Eyes. 2 300 times. 3 Organ donor. 4 True. 5 Yes. 6 Liver.

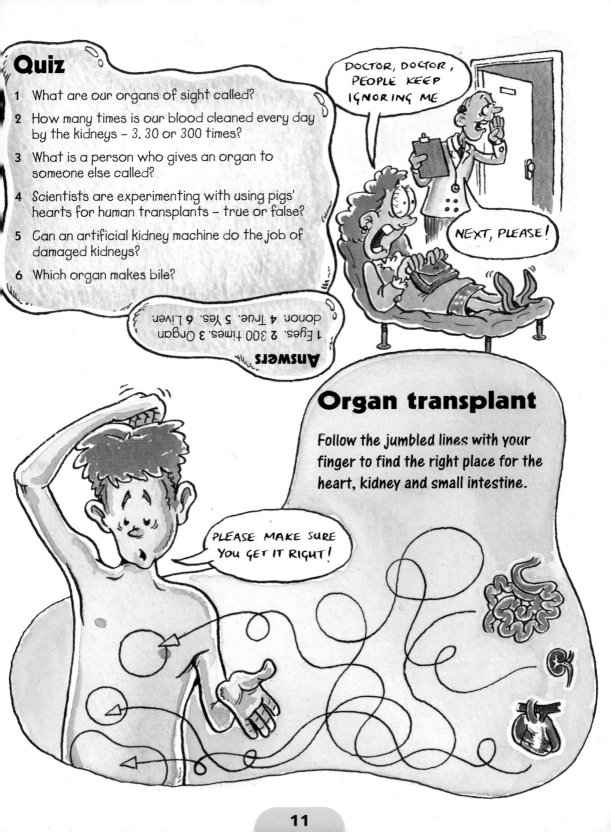

DOCTOR, DOCTOR, PEOPLE KEEP IGNORING ME

NEXT, PLEASE!

# Organ transplant

Follow the jumbled lines with your finger to find the right place for the heart, kidney and small intestine.

PLEASE MAKE SURE YOU GET IT RIGHT!

# BLOOD

The blood in our body carries oxygen from the air we breathe, as well as goodness from the food we eat. It travels in small tubes, called blood vessels, to all parts of the body. Blood is pumped around the body by a powerful muscle called the heart.

aorta

heart

artery

vein

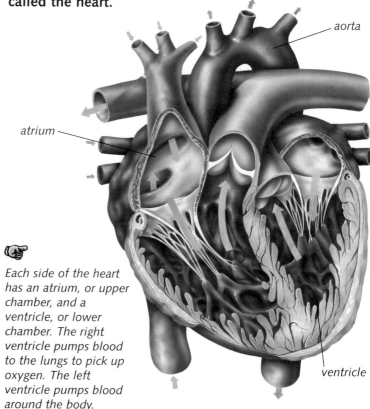

aorta

atrium

ventricle

👉 *Each side of the heart has an atrium, or upper chamber, and a ventricle, or lower chamber. The right ventricle pumps blood to the lungs to pick up oxygen. The left ventricle pumps blood around the body.*

## Quiz

1  Which fruit has a similar shape to the heart?
2  The heart lies slightly to which side of your chest?
3  There are three major blood groups – true or false?
4  When you run about, does your heart beat faster or slower?
5  What makes up 90 % of plasma?
6  What are tiny blood vessels called?

Although our blood looks red, it is mainly made up of a yellowish liquid called plasma. There are three different sorts of cells in the plasma: red cells, which carry oxygen; white cells, which help the body fight disease; and platelets, which help cuts to heal.

red blood cells

white blood cells

platelets

# Hear the heartbeat

1. To make your own stethoscope, cut the top end off two plastic bottles to make cups.

2. Then push the ends of some hosepipe or other plastic tubing into the two cups.

3. Put one cup over a friend's heart and the other cup over your ear. Can you hear the heartbeat?

## Factfile

- Blood travels away from the heart in blood vessels called arteries (coloured red in our illustration). It travels back to the heart in veins (blue).

- An adult has about five litres of blood.

- An adult's heart pumps more than 7,000 litres of blood around the body every day.

- A substance in red blood cells called haemoglobin makes blood look red.

- A child's heart beats about a hundred times each minute.

BOOM!

BOOM!

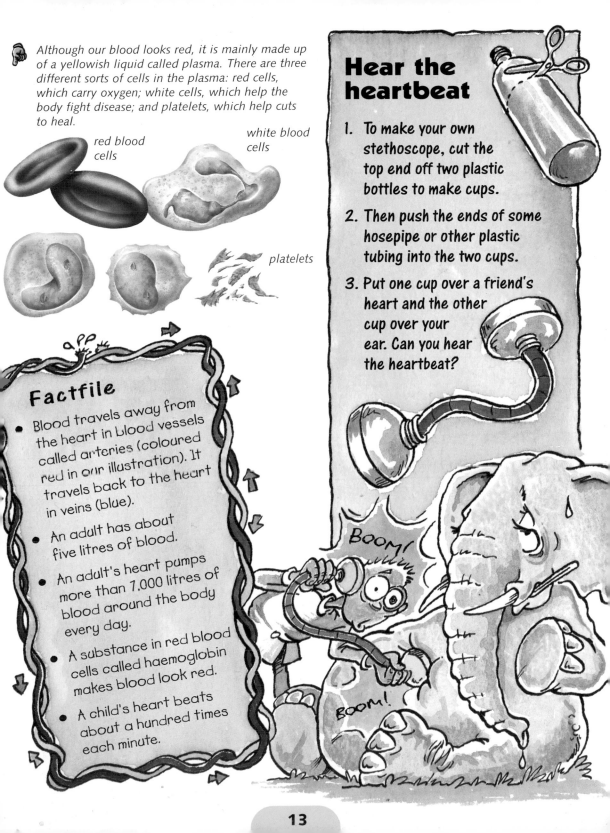

13

# BREATHING

When we breathe in, we take air into our body. Air contains a gas called oxygen, and we need this to help make our bodies work. The air we breathe in goes into our lungs, which take the oxygen into very narrow tubes and pass it into our bloodstream. When we breathe out again, the lungs get rid of used air.

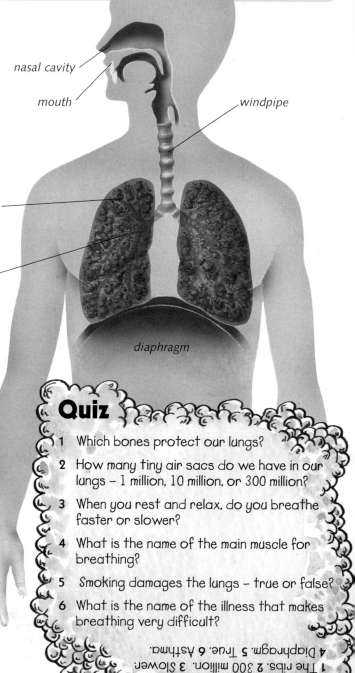

nasal cavity

mouth

windpipe

lung

bronchial tube

diaphragm

IMAGINE BREATHING IN AND OUT THOUSANDS OF TIMES A DAY. IT MAKES ME FEEL TIRED OUT!

## Quiz

1   Which bones protect our lungs?

2   How many tiny air sacs do we have in our lungs – 1 million, 10 million, or 300 million?

3   When you rest and relax, do you breathe faster or slower?

4   What is the name of the main muscle for breathing?

5   Smoking damages the lungs – true or false?

6   What is the name of the illness that makes breathing very difficult?

**Answers**
1 The ribs. 2 300 million. 3 Slower. 4 Diaphragm. 5 True. 6 Asthma.

## Breathing in and out

*As you breathe in, your rib cage expands and a large dome of muscle, called the diaphragm, contracts and flattens. The lungs then fill up with air.* ☞

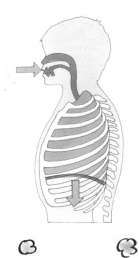

☞ *When you breathe out, the diaphragm relaxes and rises, forcing air out of the lungs.*

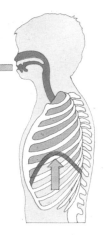

## Factfile

- An adult's lungs hold about five litres of air.
- About 21 percent of air is oxygen, which is what our body's cells need most.
- Adults usually breathe about 18 times a minute, or more than 25,000 times a day (or more than nine million times a year!).
- An adult's lungs contain about 300 billion tiny blood vessels, or capillaries; if you laid them end to end, they would stretch over 2,000 km.

## Blow football

1. Build matchboxes or building bricks into goalposts, at either end of a table. Put more boxes or bricks along the edge of the table to stop the ball rolling off.

2. Divide the players into teams (one-a-side will do), and give each player a drinking straw. Put a ping-pong ball in the middle of the table. At the first whistle the players try to blow the ball into their opponent's goal.

3. How many goals can you score before running out of puff?

# MAKING SOUNDS

**A**ll sounds are made by things vibrating, and our voices make sounds by vibrating the vocal cords. These cords are soft flaps in the larynx, or voice box, which is at the back of the throat. When air passes over the vocal cords, they vibrate and make a sound. We then use our tongue and lips to change the sounds and form words.

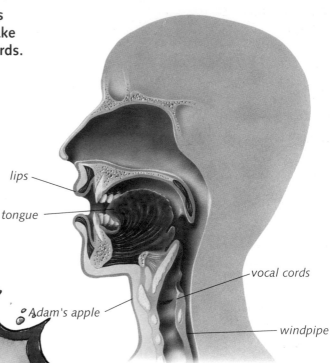

lips

tongue

vocal cords

Adam's apple

windpipe

## Factfile

• We cough when something irritates our airways; a cough can release air at up to 100 km/h.

• The Adam's apple (officially, thyroid cartilage) was supposedly called this because a piece of apple got stuck in Adam's throat when he ate the forbidden fruit.

• The noise of snoring is made by the soft part of the roof of the mouth (or palate) vibrating.

# Make a loudhailer

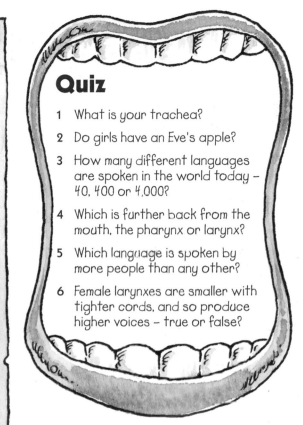

1. Bend a thin piece of cardboard (about 40 x 30 cm) into a cone shape and fix it with sticky tape.

2. Cut out a smaller piece of cardboard to cover the gap in the cone. Put it in place and then tape it.

3. Cut both ends of the cone into a neat circle. Now you can use your loudhailer as an amplifier (but warn the neighbours first!).

## Quiz

1 What is your trachea?

2 Do girls have an Eve's apple?

3 How many different languages are spoken in the world today – 40, 400 or 4,000?

4 Which is further back from the mouth, the pharynx or larynx?

5 Which language is spoken by more people than any other?

6 Female larynxes are smaller with tighter cords, and so produce higher voices – true or false?

**Answers**

1 Your windpipe. 2 No. 3 4,000. 4 Larynx.
5 Chinese. 6 True.

## Vocal cords

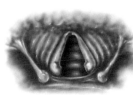

When the cords are apart, air can move freely past them and no sound is made.

Tiny muscles pull the cords together, leaving a small gap. As air is forced through the gap, the cords vibrate and make sounds.

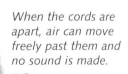

CAN YOU WHISTLE?

PHEEPP

# BRAIN

The brain, inside our skull, is the body's control centre. It keeps other parts of the body working properly, and is responsible for thoughts, feelings and memory. The brain is linked to the rest of the body by nerves. It receives information in the form of tiny electric currents. The brain 'reads' the information faster and more efficiently than any computer, and then acts on it by sending information back down the nerves.

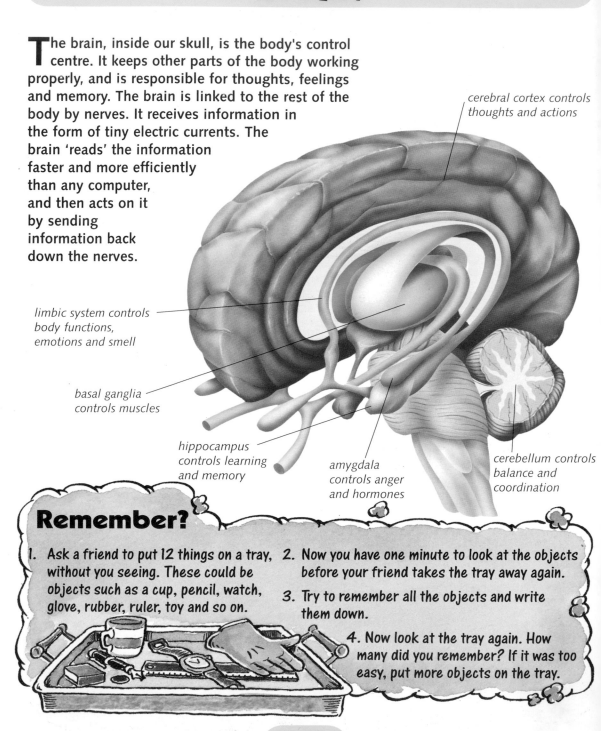

*cerebral cortex controls thoughts and actions*

*limbic system controls body functions, emotions and smell*

*basal ganglia controls muscles*

*hippocampus controls learning and memory*

*amygdala controls anger and hormones*

*cerebellum controls balance and coordination*

## Remember?

1. Ask a friend to put 12 things on a tray, without you seeing. These could be objects such as a cup, pencil, watch, glove, rubber, ruler, toy and so on.

2. Now you have one minute to look at the objects before your friend takes the tray away again.

3. Try to remember all the objects and write them down.

4. Now look at the tray again. How many did you remember? If it was too easy, put more objects on the tray.

## Factfile

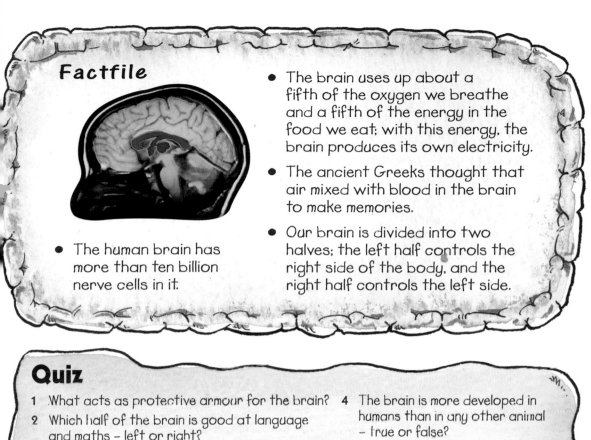

- The human brain has more than ten billion nerve cells in it.

- The brain uses up about a fifth of the oxygen we breathe and a fifth of the energy in the food we eat; with this energy, the brain produces its own electricity.

- The ancient Greeks thought that air mixed with blood in the brain to make memories.

- Our brain is divided into two halves; the left half controls the right side of the body, and the right half controls the left side.

## Quiz

1 What acts as protective armour for the brain?

2 Which half of the brain is good at language and maths – left or right?

3 Which half of the brain is good at art and music – left or right?

4 The brain is more developed in humans than in any other animal – True or false?

5 When we are asleep, does the brain go on working?

6 What send messages to the brain along optic nerves?

THE LEFT HALF OF THE BRAIN IS GOOD AT LOGICAL THINKING.

AND THE RIGHT HALF IS GOOD AT ART.

**Answers**
1 The skull.
2 Left 3 Right
4 True. 5 Yes.
6 The eyes.

# NERVOUS SYSTEM

A network of nerves runs throughout your whole body. They connect the brain – the body's control centre – to the spinal cord, which runs down the body inside the backbone. Together, the brain and spinal cord make up the body's central nervous system. Smaller nerves run from the spinal cord all over the body. The nerves send messages to and from the brain, giving information about the senses.

## Reflex action

*If you touch a sharp pin, a message goes along a sensory nerve to your spinal cord. A motor nerve then moves your hand away at once. This immediate response is called a reflex action. The message carries on to your brain, which knows about the pain after your hand has moved, so then you feel it.*

## Factfile

- The medulla lies between the lower part of the brain and the top of the spinal cord; its nerve cells carry messages between the two.

- In adults, the spinal cord is about 40 cm long.

- The spinal cord runs inside the backbone, and the vertebrae that make up the backbone protect it.

- If the spinal cord is broken in an accident, the person is paralyzed because the nerves' messages cannot get through to the brain.

# Quiz

1  Is the forebrain at the front or the back?

2  What are neurones?

3  What does CNS stand for?

4  Are humans vertebrates or invertebrates?

5  Can people move as fast as their own nerves' messages?

6  Nerves are in charge of muscles – true or false?

**Answers**

1 Front 2 Nerve cells. 3 Central nervous system. 4 Vertebrates (they have a backbone). 5 No. 6 True.

# Make a reactometer

1. Divide a long strip of stiff card into seven equal parts. Make each section a different colour.

2. Ask a friend to hold the strip above your hand.

3. Place your thumb and index finger just below the strip and try to pinch the strip as quickly as possible when your friend lets go of it. The closer you catch it to the bottom end, the better your reactions are.

4. Now swap places and test your friend's reactions.

MESSAGES TRAVEL ALONG NERVES AT 400 KILOMETRES AN HOUR.

JUST AS WELL!

21

# SLEEP

Most people spend about a third of their lives asleep. Sleep gives the body time to rest, which is why we sleep more than usual when we are ill. Since muscles have very little work to do when we are asleep, the parts of the brain that control movement can rest too.

We grow when we are asleep, so babies need at least 18 hours of sleep every day. As we get older and grow less, we sleep less.

## Quiz

1  Does your heart beat faster or more slowly when you are asleep?

2  What are scary dreams called?

3  What is the name of the fairy-tale character who slept for twenty years?

4  What type of clock wakes people up?

5  Do old people usually need a lot or little sleep?

6  What does REM stand for?

**Answers**
1 More slowly. 2 Nightmares.
3 Rip Van Winkle. 4 Alarm clock.
5 Little. 6 Rapid eye movement.

*In the traditional tale, Rip Van Winkle falls into a deep sleep for 20 years. When he finally wakes up, he can't understand why the world is so different.*

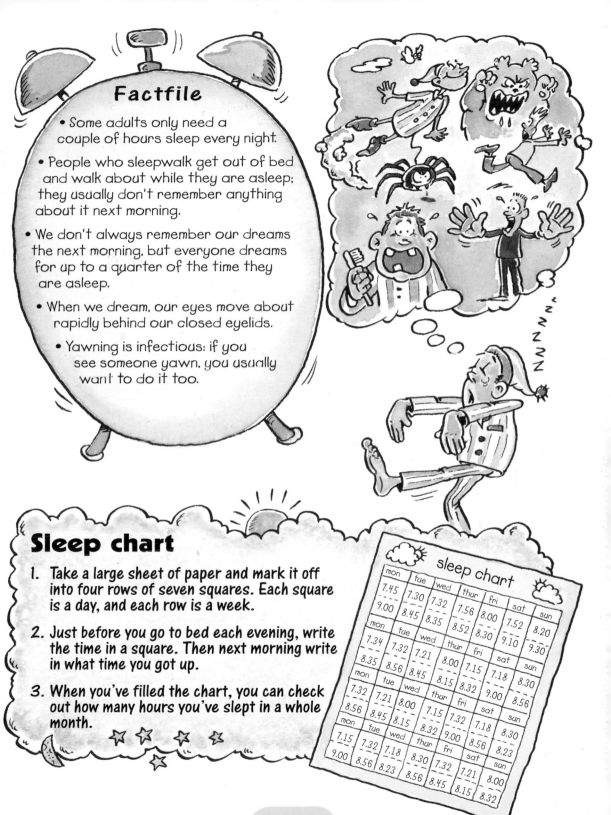

## Factfile

• Some adults only need a couple of hours sleep every night.

• People who sleepwalk get out of bed and walk about while they are asleep; they usually don't remember anything about it next morning.

• We don't always remember our dreams the next morning, but everyone dreams for up to a quarter of the time they are asleep.

• When we dream, our eyes move about rapidly behind our closed eyelids.

• Yawning is infectious: if you see someone yawn, you usually want to do it too.

# Sleep chart

1. Take a large sheet of paper and mark it off into four rows of seven squares. Each square is a day, and each row is a week.

2. Just before you go to bed each evening, write the time in a square. Then next morning write in what time you got up.

3. When you've filled the chart, you can check out how many hours you've slept in a whole month.

### sleep chart

| mon | tue | wed | thur | fri | sat | sun |
|-----|-----|-----|------|-----|-----|-----|
| 7.45 | 7.30 | 7.32 | 7.56 | 8.00 | 7.52 | 8.20 |
| 9.00 | 8.45 | 8.35 | 8.52 | 8.30 | 9.10 | 9.30 |
| 7.34 | 7.32 | 7.21 | 8.00 | 7.15 | 7.18 | 8.30 |
| 8.35 | 8.56 | 8.45 | 8.15 | 8.32 | 9.00 | 8.56 |
| 7.32 | 7.21 | 8.00 | 7.15 | 7.32 | 7.18 | 8.30 |
| 8.56 | 8.45 | 8.15 | 8.32 | 9.00 | 8.56 | 8.23 |
| 7.15 | 7.32 | 7.18 | 8.30 | 7.32 | 7.21 | 8.00 |
| 9.00 | 8.56 | 8.23 | 8.56 | 8.45 | 8.15 | 8.32 |

# SKIN

The skin is our body's protection from the outside world. It keeps out dirt, water and germs, as well as shielding us from the Sun's burning rays. Much of our body is made of water, and the skin stops the body from drying out.

Our skin is full of nerve endings, which send messages to the brain with information about such important things as pain, heat and cold. 👉

*The inner layer, called the dermis, contains masses of nerve endings.*

👉 *The tough outer layer of the skin, called the epidermis, is waterproof and germ-proof.*

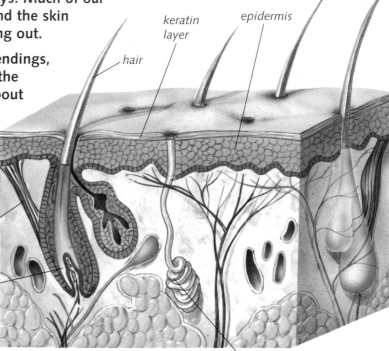

keratin layer

epidermis

hair

hair erector muscle

hair follicle

sweat gland

## Quiz

1  What are little brown sun-spots on the skin called?

2  Do our fingers give ten different fingerprints?

3  What is a skin specialist called?

4  Do you sweat more when you're hot or cold?

5  Skin colour comes from a substance called lanolin – true or false?

6  Do you shiver when you're hot or cold?

*Every single person in the whole world has slightly different fingerprints.*

arch

loop

whorl

DON'T FORGET TO CHECK OUT THE ARCHES AND LOOPS.

# Hand and foot prints

1. Use ready-mixed paint thickened with a little PVA glue and paint your palms and fingers with it. Then press your hands down firmly on a sheet of paper.

2. Wash your hands then roll out a long strip of paper on the floor. Take off your shoes and socks and step into a tray of the paint. Then walk to the other end of the paper.

3. Compare your prints with a friend's. Can you see the difference? Use a magnifying glass for a really close look.

## Factfile

- The thickest skin (about 3 mm) is on the palms of your hands and soles of your feet.

- We sweat to keep cool; produced by glands in the dermis, sweat takes heat from the body and helps cool it down as it dries on the skin.

- We get goose bumps when tiny hairs stand up and pull the skin up around them; the hairs help keep you warm by trapping air next to your skin.

I'M VERY THICK SKINNED

# HAIR AND NAILS

 We have hair all over our bodies, except on the palms of our hands and the soles of our feet. Most of the hairs are too fine and tiny to see properly. Hairs give our skin extra warmth and protection. The hair on our head grows thickest and longest.

Our nails are there to protect the tips of our fingers and toes. Both nails and hair are made from a tough substance called keratin.

Wavy hair grows from oval follicles.

Hairs grow from follicles in the dermis of the skin.

Curly hair grows from rectangular follicles.

Straight hair grows from round follicles.

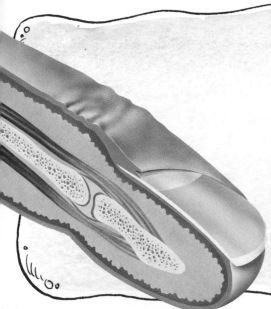

## Factfile

- Nails grow from the base, under the skin; the pale half-moon is new nail that has just grown.

- An Indian man grew all his fingernails to over a metre long.

- The hair on your head grows about 3 mm each week, or 15 cm a year.

- Most fair-haired people have about 140,000 hairs on their head; people with brown hair have about 120,000; and redheads have just 90,000.

- About 50 hairs fall out of a person's head every day.

# Quiz

1. Hair colour comes from a substance called gelatine – true or false?

2. How long do nails usually grow in a month – 1, 3 or 7 mm?

3. Do babies have fingernails before they are born?

4. Was the world's longest beard over 1, 3 or 5 m long?

5. Does a haircut hurt?

6. What is the thin strip of skin at the base of a nail called?

EEK!

I'D BE HAPPY WITH ANY KIND OF HAIR!

# Green hair

1. Cut the top off a pumpkin and scoop out some of the flesh. Fill the pumpkin with a layer of cotton wool.

2. Moisten the cotton wool with water and sow cress seeds on it. Now draw a happy face on your pumpkin with black marker pen.

3. Keep the seeds and seedlings watered and watch your pumpkin's green hair grow.

27

# TEETH

Our teeth do a very important job. They break food down into small pieces, so that it is ready for swallowing. Teeth have three different shapes, which are designed to do different jobs. The sharp incisors at the front bite into food and cut it up. The pointed canine teeth tear tough food. And the big molars at the back grind and mash our food.

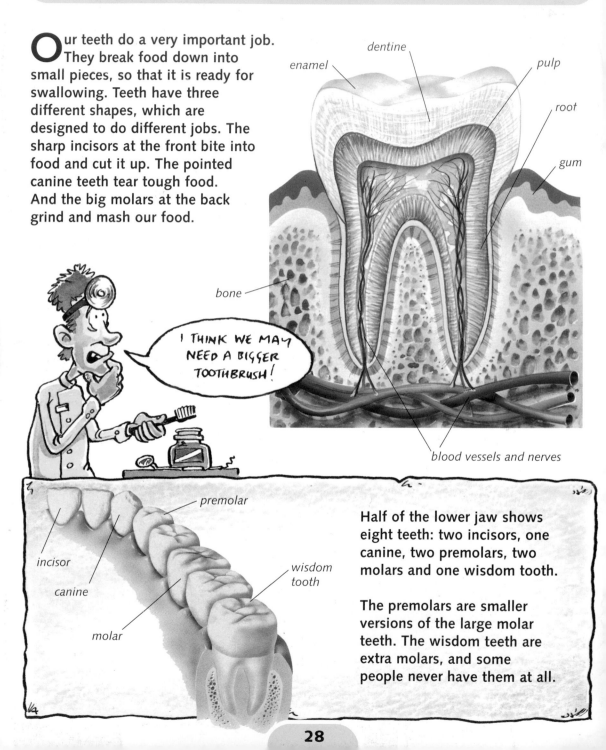

I THINK WE MAY NEED A BIGGER TOOTHBRUSH!

enamel

dentine

pulp

root

gum

bone

blood vessels and nerves

premolar

incisor

canine

molar

wisdom tooth

Half of the lower jaw shows eight teeth: two incisors, one canine, two premolars, two molars and one wisdom tooth.

The premolars are smaller versions of the large molar teeth. The wisdom teeth are extra molars, and some people never have them at all.

# Quiz

1 What can you wear on your teeth to make them straight?

2 What are a young child's first teeth called?

3 What is caries?

4 Are people with wisdom teeth really wiser?

5 What is a tooth doctor called?

6 New-born babies don't usually have teeth – true or false?

**Answers**

1 A brace. 2 Milk teeth. 3 Tooth decay. 4 No (though they disagree!) 5 Dentist 6 True.

# Egg decay

1. This an experiment to see how acid can attack your teeth if it is left untouched.

2. Put an eggshell into a small glass or jar of vinegar (which is an acid). Leave it for a couple of days to see what happens.

3. Now you can see why it's good to brush your teeth!

I.O.U.

OH NO, I'VE FORGOTTEN MY PURSE. I'LL HAVE TO LEAVE AN IOU.

# Factfile

- Children lose their first set of 20 milk teeth, which start to fall out when they are five or six.

- Adults have 28 permanent teeth, and some get an extra four wisdom teeth at the back.

- If sugar and bacteria are left on the teeth for long, they can produce acid and cause tooth decay; that's why it's important to brush your teeth regularly.

- Some people grow a third set of teeth (though this is very rare).

# DIGESTION

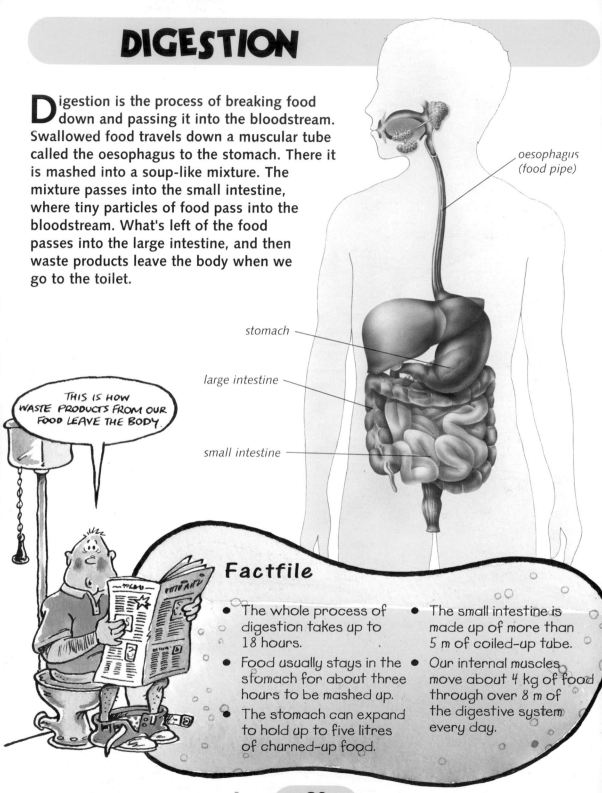

**D**igestion is the process of breaking food down and passing it into the bloodstream. Swallowed food travels down a muscular tube called the oesophagus to the stomach. There it is mashed into a soup-like mixture. The mixture passes into the small intestine, where tiny particles of food pass into the bloodstream. What's left of the food passes into the large intestine, and then waste products leave the body when we go to the toilet.

oesophagus
(food pipe)

stomach

large intestine

small intestine

THIS IS HOW WASTE PRODUCTS FROM OUR FOOD LEAVE THE BODY.

## Factfile

- The whole process of digestion takes up to 18 hours.

- Food usually stays in the stomach for about three hours to be mashed up.

- The stomach can expand to hold up to five litres of churned-up food.

- The small intestine is made up of more than 5 m of coiled-up tube.

- Our internal muscles move about 4 kg of food through over 8 m of the digestive system every day.

START HERE

# Find the food

Enter the maze with your finger, and see if you can find your way to a tasty meal.

# Quiz

1  What carries the energy from food to all parts of the body?

2  Which is longer, the large or small intestine?

3  What is liquid waste called?

4  Which is wider, the large or small intestine?

5  Does chewing food well help digestion?

6  The stomach is an expandable organ – true or false?

DON'T FORGET TO CHEW AT LEAST 40 TIMES!

**Answers**

1 Blood. 2 Small intestine. 3 Urine. 4 Large intestine. 5 Yes. 6 True.

# FOOD AND DRINK

Our bodies need important substances, called nutrients, which we get from food and drink. These nutrients help us to grow and help the body repair damaged cells, as well as providing energy. We need energy to live and be active.

*It is important that we have a balanced diet, so that we don't miss out on any essential nutrients. This means we must eat food from various groups – carbohydrates, proteins, fats and fibre, as well as vitamins and minerals. They are all useful in different ways.*

carbohydrates

proteins

fats

fibre

vitamins and minerals

### Factfile

- Carbohydrates give us the sort of instant energy that we can use very quickly.

- Proteins are used to make body cells and they help us stay strong.

- Fats give us energy that can be stored by the body to be used later.

- Fibre helps other foods pass more easily through the digestive system.

- The body also needs lots of water – to make blood and sweat, and to carry wastes from the body in urine.

## Quiz

1 Which vitamin do oranges give us lots of?

2 Which English cheese comes from the same place as a famous gorge?

3 Which drink has lots of calcium?

4 Which food group does pasta belong to?

5 What is milk without fat called?

6 What are wheat, barley and maize?

**Answers**

1 Vitamin C. 2 Cheddar. 3 Milk.
4 Carbohydrates. 5 Skimmed milk.
6 Cereals.

WE'RE EATING A BALANCED MEAL!

## Salad face

1. Healthy foods can be fun.

2. Salad girl's face is made of mashed potatoes spread out on a plate, hard-boiled eggs, tomatoes, parsley, cress, cucumber, carrots and radishes.

3. With her long chive eyelashes, olive eyes and curly lettuce hair, she's almost too good to eat.

# SMELL AND TASTE

Smell and taste are both very important senses. Our sense of smell is much stronger than that of taste. When we smell something, tiny scent particles go into our nose, which sends messages along a special nerve to the brain. When we taste food, we rely on its smell and texture to give us information about it. The tongue also sends messages to the brain. So when we eat something, the tongue and nose combine to help us enjoy it.

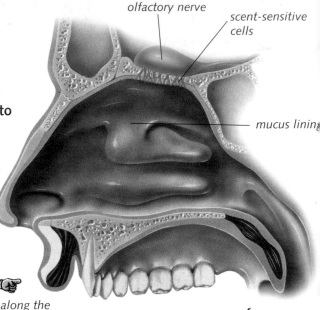

olfactory nerve

scent-sensitive cells

mucus lining

Scent particles dissolve in the mucus lining, and the cells at the top of the nose send signals along the olfactory (or smelling) nerve. This leads to a special part of the brain.

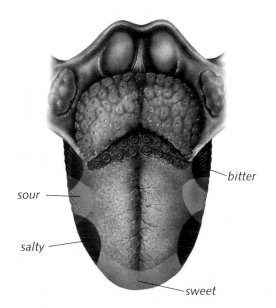

bitter

sour

salty

sweet

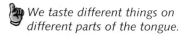 We taste different things on different parts of the tongue.

GAGA SMELL!

## Factfile

- When we sneeze, we clear the nose of unwanted particles, such as dust; the explosive rush of air made by a sneeze can reach 160 km/h!

- There are about 10,000 taste buds on our tongue; they are tiny sense organs that help us taste things.

- Babies have taste buds all over the inside of their mouth, and they are very sensitive to smells.

- When you have a cold, you can't taste food properly; this is because your nose is blocked and you can't smell much.

# Quiz

1 Which sense is stronger, smell or taste?

2 Does honey taste bitter or sweet?

3 Dogs have a better sense of smell than people – true or false?

4 Does a big nose smell more than a small nose?

5 What does the olfactory area of the brain specialize in?

6 Which taste do we get from the tip of the tongue?

**Answers**

1 Smell. 2 Sweet 3 True. 4 No. 5 Smells. 6 Sweet

CALL YOURSELF A SNIFFER DOG!

SNIFF! SNIFF!

# Testing taste

1. See how well you can taste things without the help of your nose.

2. Cut an apple, a carrot and some hard cheese into small pieces.

3. Cover your eyes with a blindfold and hold your nose while a friend gives you the pieces of food one by one. Can you tell which is which by taste? Now try the same with other foods.

# HEARING

Sound waves travel through the air. The outer part of our ear – the part we can see – is shaped to collect the sound waves and pass them into the auditory canal. All sounds are made by things vibrating, and inside the ear the sound waves make a thin sheet of skin, called the eardrum, vibrate. The vibrations are passed on further until nerve endings pick them up and send messages to the brain, so that we 'hear' the sounds.

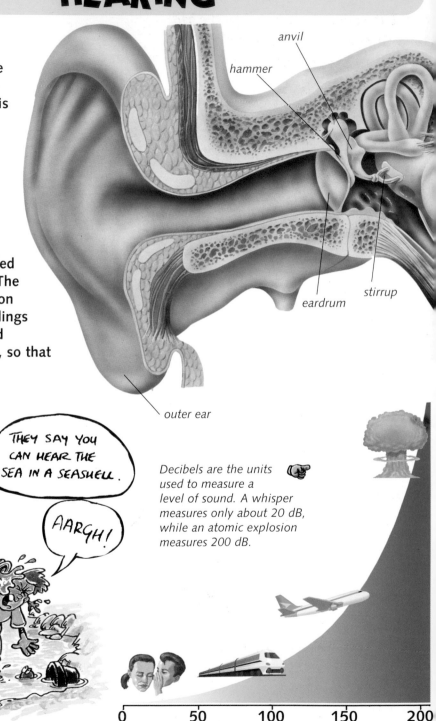

anvil

hammer

stirrup

eardrum

outer ear

THEY SAY YOU CAN HEAR THE SEA IN A SEASHELL.

AARGH!

*Decibels are the units used to measure a level of sound. A whisper measures only about 20 dB, while an atomic explosion measures 200 dB.*

0     50     100     150     200

# Ear-drum

1. Cut a large sheet from a plastic bag. Stretch the sheet over a big tin and put a rubber band around it.

2. Sprinkle sugar onto the plastic.

3. Hold a metal tray next to the drum and beat it with a wooden spoon.

4. The grains of sugar will hop and jump as your drum vibrates with the sound. Just like a real eardrum!

cochlea

## Factfile

- The cochlea contains a fluid which moves tiny hairs that send signals to the brain.

- Sometimes our ears 'pop' in a plane or lift; this happens when air pressure outside changes and is equalized in the middle ear.

- The tubular canals next to the cochlea let the brain know what movements the body is making and so help us with balance.

- Sound travels at about 1,225 km/h.

## Quiz

1 Do sound messages travel along the auditory or the oral nerve?

2 Which is the smallest bone in the ear (and the whole body)?

3 Dogs hear a greater range of sounds than humans – true or false?

4 Is your balance better or worse when your ears are blocked?

5 Which world-famous German composer was deaf?

6 Which of the ear bones is the incus?

**Answers**
1 Auditory.
2 Stirrup bone.
3 True. 4 Worse.
5 Beethoven.
6 Anvil bone.

# SEEING

We see through our eyes. When light comes into each eye, it passes through a lens, which bends it very precisely. The light rays form an image on an area at the back of the eye called the retina. This image is upside down. Light-sensitive cells in the retina send messages along nerves to the brain. The brain then turns the image around so that we see things the right way up.

*When there is very bright light, our pupils are small. But when there is less light, the pupils open more and grow bigger, to let more light in.*

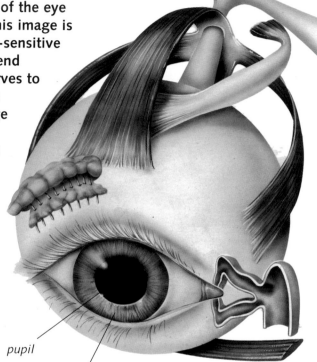

retina

optic nerve

pupil

iris

# Experience the blind spot

1. Cover your left eye and look at the dog.

2. Now move the book slowly towards you. What happens to the cat? It should disappear and then reappear, as it passes the blind spot.

3. Try the same experiment, but this time move the book away from you.

*THAT BULL MUST BE COLOUR-BLIND!*

cornea

lens

iris

## Factfile

- Some people find it difficult to tell the difference between colours, especially red and green; we call this colour blindness.

- Our eyes are about the size of ping-pong balls.

- The coloured part of our eye is called the iris; we inherit the colour of our eyes from our parents.

- You normally blink about 15 times each minute (to keep the eyes moist and clean).

# TOUCHING

Our sense of touch gives us a lot of information about the world, allowing us to learn about things around us without seeing them. When we touch things, nerve endings under the surface of the skin send instant messages to the brain. Our brain interprets the messages, and we feel things – such as hardness or softness, or heat or cold, as well as pain or pleasurable sensations.

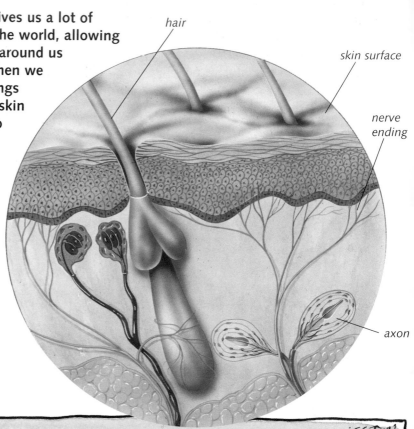

hair

skin surface

nerve ending

axon

Nerve endings lie just beneath the surface of the skin. They send messages to the central nervous system along threadlike axons.

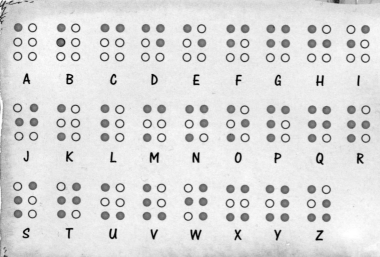

A B C D E F G H I
J K L M N O P Q R
S T U V W X Y Z

Blind people can read by using a system called Braille. The letters of their special alphabet are raised dots that the fingers can touch and feel.

# Quiz

1 Does a special part of the brain deal with touch?

2 Many keyboards have raised dots so that typists can feel where their fingers are – true or false?

3 What is a typist who can type without looking at the keys called?

4 Is our sense of touch generally less sensitive in cold weather?

5 What is the name for a computer monitor that operates by touch?

6 Are some people more sensitive to pain than others?

**Answers**

1 Yes (the parietal lobe).
2 True. 3 Touch-typist. 4 Yes.
5 Touch screen.
6 Yes (according to researchers).

OOH STOP IT, THAT TICKLES!

# Factfile

- The Braille system was named after its French inventor, Louis Braille (1809-52), who went blind at the age of three and later became an organ player and a professor.

- We have most nerve endings beneath our fingertips, and the soles of our feet also have many nerves.

- We feel pain to stay safe; it's like an alarm that goes off to tell us that something is wrong.

# Play it by feel

1. Collect lots of objects that feel and look different: a sweet, feather, apple, biscuit, ball, stone and so on.

2. Put a blindfold over your friend's eyes and ask him or her to describe the objects just by touching them. Can they guess what each object is?

3. Now ask your friend to put together a different collection so that you can play it by feel.

# HOW BABIES GROW

**E**ach of us began life as a tiny cell inside our mother's body. One of our father's cells joined up with one of our mother's egg-cells. The egg-cell then divided to make more cells and kept on growing to make a baby.

Babies grow in a special part of a mother's body called the womb. As the baby gets bigger, the pregnant mother's womb stretches. After about nine months, the baby is ready to be born.

5 weeks

8 weeks

*The fertilized cell develops into an embryo. After eight weeks, the growing embryo is called a foetus.*

12 weeks

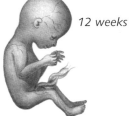

20 weeks

40 weeks

30 weeks

## Quiz

1   Are two twins always the same sex?
2   What are five babies born together called?
3   What is the name of the cord that connects a mother to her growing baby?
4   What's the proper word for tummy button?
5   Which organs produce a woman's egg cells?
6   A person specially trained to help women in childbirth is called a midwife – true or false?

**Answers**

1 No. 2 Quintuplets. 3 Umbilical cord. 4 Navel. 5 Ovaries. 6 True.

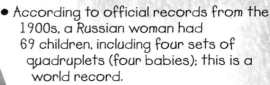

- According to official records from the 1900s, a Russian woman had 69 children, including four sets of quadruplets (four babies); this is a world record.

  - After about eight weeks in the womb, a growing baby has all its important body organs, although it is only 4 cm long.

  - Inside the womb a baby floats in a watery fluid and gets food and oxygen from its mother through a special cord.

*Triplets are three brothers or sisters who develop from three eggs fertilized at the same time.*

THREE BABIES BORN TOGETHER ARE CALLED TRIPLETS.

# Spot the difference

There are six differences between these two twins.

Can you find them all?

# GROWING UP

Tiny babies cannot look after themselves, so they need lots of love and care. But they grow and learn very quickly, first crawling and then taking their first proper steps. By the time a child is two years old, it can do a lot of things for itself. By then the child is already half the height it will be as an adult.

## Factfile

- The world's tallest person was American Robert Wadlow; he was taller than most adults by the age of ten, and finally reached a height of 2.72 m.

- The tallest woman was Zeng Jinlian, of China, who measured 2.48 m.

- The oldest person in the world was Frenchwoman Jeanne Calment, who died in 1997 at the age of 122.

- Adults slow up as they get older because their bodies do not use energy as efficiently and their cells cannot replace themselves as quickly.

I'd love to meet someone over two metres tall!

As children go on to become teenagers and young adults, they also grow more independent and start to make all their own decisions. As adults, they may leave their parents and eventually have children of their own.

# Height chart

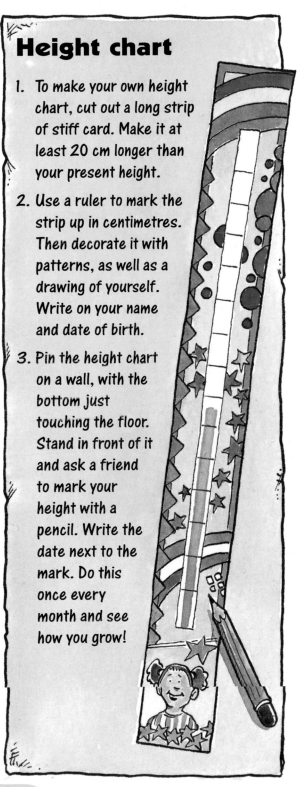

1. To make your own height chart, cut out a long strip of stiff card. Make it at least 20 cm longer than your present height.

2. Use a ruler to mark the strip up in centimetres. Then decorate it with patterns, as well as a drawing of yourself. Write on your name and date of birth.

3. Pin the height chart on a wall, with the bottom just touching the floor. Stand in front of it and ask a friend to mark your height with a pencil. Write the date next to the mark. Do this once every month and see how you grow!

# KEEPING HEALTHY

To stay healthy, we have to look after our bodies. We must make sure that we eat properly, take lots of exercise and get as much sleep and rest as we need. We must also wash and stay clean.

Sometimes there is nothing you can do to stop yourself falling ill. But if you normally lead a healthy life, you will probably get better much more quickly than if you didn't.

*Stretching your muscles before exercise can help to prevent injury.*

*Dancing and other similar activities can help to make you more supple and improve your stamina.*

## Factfile

- Today we can have vaccinations to stop us getting certain diseases; this gives us a mild, harmless form of the disease that builds up our resistance.

- People today live much longer than they ever did in the past, especially in the richer parts of the world.

- Smoking cigarettes, drinking too much alcohol and taking any non-medical drugs all damage the body and can ruin your health.

# Quiz

1 What is the name for vigorous exercises that help the body increase its intake of oxygen?

2 Which vehicle takes people to hospital in an emergency?

3 What is an arachnophobic person afraid of?

4 Which country has the most hospitals?

5 What does a doctor write out to give us medicine?

6 Which sport is played with a shuttlecock?

**Answers**

1 Aerobics. 2 An ambulance. 3 Spiders. 4 China. 5 A prescription. 6 Badminton.

DANCING IS SUCH GOOD EXERCISE!

# Warming up

It's very important to warm your muscles up before you do strenuous exercise. Here are some good ways to warm up. Do each of them five times.

1. Stretch your arms above your head, then squat and swing your arms between your legs

2. Pull each knee in turn up towards your chest (this is good for your knees, thighs and hips.

3. With legs slightly apart, lift each arm in turn and bend towards the other side.

# Index